CHRISTMAS 1990.

From - Kathy

To - Bruce.

THE
TURBO
DECADE

THE
TURBO
DECADE

Photographs and text by

Behram Kapadia

For Alex and James

Acknowledgements

The author wishes to thank all the people who have given their help and support during this project, particularly Nicholas Collins at Osprey for his enthusiasm and guidance, Tim Parker at Motorbooks International for his sponsorship, and David Tremayne at Motoring News for allowing access to much-needed information. John Pitchforth and Susie Keane must also be thanked for staging the author's Grand Prix photographic exhibition at the Nikon Gallery, thereby providing the exposure which led to this book. Finally, Behram Kapadia wishes to say 'thank you' to his wife, Sally, for her patience, and their two sons, Alexis and James, for sharing his enthusiasm for Grand Prix racing.

Published in 1990 by Osprey Publishing
59 Grosvenor Street
London W1X 9DA

© Behram Kapadia 1990

British Library in Cataloguing in Publication Data

Kapadia, Behram
  Turbo decade
  I. Formula 1 racing cars. Racing. Races: Grand Prix, history
  I. Title
  796.72

ISBN 0-85045-995-9

Editor Nicholas Collins
Design Behram Kapadia

Printed in Hong Kong

Half-title page
Alboreto driving the uncompetitive Ferrari 156/85 in the 1985 European Grand Prix

Title page
Alain Prost driving the Renault RE40 passes under the Dunlop Bridge at the top of Hailwood Hill, Brands Hatch, 1985

▷ In this day of high-tech computerised lap counting and time-keeping it is refreshing to see a human face behind manually-operated sign boards

Contents

The Early Years

$\mathbf{T}$urbocharged! The word itself suggests adrenalin being pumped into the system. To the archetypal man or woman in the street it conjures up resentful images of a souped-up car – perhaps it was a Saab 900 or a Renault 5 which spectacularly carved-up the Cortina or Marina that he or she was driving. Certainly in the late 1970s these two cars were the most commonly available (although Porsche did introduce a Turbo Carrera model as early as 1973). Both reinforced injury to a following driver's ego because they had a 'Turbo' badge on their boot lids which you glimpsed fleetingly before they vanished into the distance. And it was these two marques which led to the explosion of the word 'Turbo' being used indiscriminately to label anything from a vacuum cleaner to hair dryer in the adman's quest to describe any branded item as more powerful than the rest.

To start this brief story of the turbo decade in Formula One Grand Prix motor racing it must be remembered that as long ago as 1950, a solitary turbocharged diesel-engined car ran at Indianapolis. This was really a lorry engine made by Cummins and with turbocharging it gave the car, made by Frank Kurtis, a decent turn of speed. The first attempt ended in failure when the turbo-drive seized. Kurtis and Cummins contested the race again in 1952 but the combination of weight, chassis build and tyres proved unsuited to each other, and again the car did not finish the race distance.

Porsche and Renault Gordini entered sports prototype cars in various guises and competitions with a view to turbocharging between 1975 and 1979. Porsche was more successful due to the unreliability of the Renault engine although it was Renault who pioneered the way in Formula One.

The architect responsible for the development of the Renault V6 Formula One engine was ex-Automobiles Alpine's engine development head, Bernard Dudot. Dudot had been headhunted by Renault Gordini, traditionally

◁ Alain Prost in the Renault RE20 turbo is flagged away for a practice lap from the end of the pit lane

the sporting and competition branch of Renault. After a lot of work, and investment by Elf-Aquitaine, the French petrol company, on different sports car engines of 2-litres and with varying results, Renault became committed to the turbocharged route. The 1.5-litre EFl Formula One engine was born in early 1976 and underwent a comprehensive testing programme but it was not until after Le Mans of that year, when, despite the unreliabilty of the works' Porsche team, a Porsche still won, that Renault's chief, Bernard Hanon, approved development of the first Renault turbocharged Formula One Grand Prix car. Yet winning Le Mans still remained Renault's number one objective.

A massive amount of development work and testing went into the Formula One project during the early part of 1977. It was at Silverstone in July 1977 that the French driver Jean-Pierre Jabouille gave the world's first turbocharged Grand Prix car its racing debut. Uninspiringly, Jabouille in his RS01 retired owing to inlet manifold problems. Renault continued competing during the 1977 season but was plagued with lack of speed and unreliability. Most other teams still preferred to put their trust in the brilliantly engineered

▷ The preparation of cars by the Ferrari team is legendary and here the pits crew have just laid out everything they need for a tyre change on Villeneuve's car

▽ Seigfrid Stohr in the Arrows A3 during practice in the pits at Silverstone

△ The 1981 TAG Saudia Williams reveals its Ford Cosworth engine

◁ Saudia Williams cars line-up in the pit lane in 1981

▷ Carlos Reutemann standing beside his Williams FW07

Cosworth DFV. This normally-aspirated masterpiece is still the most successful ever Formula One engine.

1978 saw a continuation of the original car/driver partnership and the South African Grand Prix at Kyalami gave an uplift to the team when Jabouille qualified sixth fastest in practice. The high altitude of the circuit favoured turbo-breathing. 1978 also gave Renault its long-awaited and aspired for victory at Le Mans. Having won the 24-hour race and got this obsession out of the way, more resources and technical expertise were poured in towards the Formula One project. More efforts at perfecting the RS01 resulted in Jabouille winning third place on the grid at Monaco and recording the fastest straight-line speed at Monza. Although unreliability, throttle lag and overweight were still problems

to overcome, the Renault came fourth at the United States Grand Prix later in the year where it won its first three World Championship points.

Still the only turbo-engined Grand Prix contenders in 1979, the new Formula One season saw an expansion of the Renault team to two cars – Jabouille being joined by Rene Arnoux, a very talented young French driver and definitely an up-and-coming Grand Prix star. Jabouille took pole position at Kyalami on this occasion, no doubt the height of the circuit again playing a part in helping the power output of the engine. With continued improvement in the season, a new chassis design, designated RS10, was tried and at the Monaco Grand Prix the engine was fitted with a twin-turbo configuration which gave a quicker reaction to the accelerator and much better flexibility.

△ Didier Pironi's Ferrari No. 28 is being retrieved by a breakdown vehicle after an excursion into the countryside

△ Mario Andretti in the 1981 normally-aspirated V12 Alfa Romeo 179C, waiting to go out on a practice lap

Even though the engine reliability was improving there were still problems with tyres, brakes and the drive-train. However, Renault turbos were on the front row of the grid in France, Britain, Germany, Austria, Holland and Italy, and the car, in the hands of Jabouille won the French Grand Prix at Dijon, its home ground, much enhancing its prestige and pointing the way things were to be in future. Leaving aside Renault's progress, 1979 would be remembered as the year when Niki Lauda and James Hunt retired from the sport and Jody Scheckter took the World Championship relying on his dependable Ferrari 312T4. Lauda, of course, returned to the sport later. 1979 must also rank as the year when the runner-up prize should have gone to a simple and uncomplicated ground effect Williams FW07 designed by Patrick Head and driven brilliantly by the hard-charging Australian Alan Jones. Lotus, meanwhile, despaired with the ill-handling 79 and unreliable 80. Brabham finally abandoned the Alfa V12 in favour of the Cosworth DFV, and Piquet managed to put in a few respectable performances at last.

1980, however, was not to be a Renault walkover. Although Jabouille was on pole at Brazil and South Africa and Arnoux at Austria, Holland and Italy; Arnoux won at Brazil and South Africa – Jabouille taking the flag at Austria only. The well-deserved World Champion that year was Alan Jones with his spirited drives in the Ford Cosworth-engined Williams FW07B. The popular Australian never came lower than third in ten of the fourteen races in 1980, a remarkable achievement. With Carlos Reutemann's support as driver number two the Frank Williams team won the Constructors' Championship with an amazing three figure score, while the French Ligier team was second. Renault's performance, although starting the season well on their Michelin tyres, deteriorated. Arnoux bravely struggled with the suspect handling. He had survived a couple of suspension failures in Canada and further difficulties with a faulty set of valve springs at Hockenheim. It was also surprising that with all the money available Renault had no spare car for either of the drivers. Ferrari,

▽ Derek Daly drove the Rizla March 811/02–03 in 1983

△ Ken Tyrrell (right) and Michele Alboreto seated in the Tyrrell 010 during practice. British Grand Prix, 1981

having seen Renault Sport's achievements in the previous year, were developing their own V6 twin overhead camshaft turbo engine and the 126C made its debut at Imola in September 1980.

During the 1981 season Gilles Villeneuve and Didier Pironi were teammates at Ferrari. With several improvements in the turbo's efficiency Ferrari and Villeneuve took pole position at San Marino and scored a popular victory at Monaco in the same month. A month later Villeneuve, with his talented, instinctive driving, charmed the car again to score a victory at Jarama in Spain. The car was not without problems. The chassis was unwieldy although sheer power (about 550 bhp as compared to the Ford Cosworth's 490 bhp) delivered from the engine was impressive enough in terms of absolute speed and overcame handling problems on the straights and under-acceleration out of the corners. A computerised fuel-metering system was installed after teething problems and the improvement was immediate. Also the KKK turbocharged Ferrari engine was

most notable for its lack of turbo lag. Ferrari's secret was to borrow from gas turbine technology, thus the engineers prevented the waste-gate side from slowing down too much when the throttles were shut and which meant quicker pick-up when the accelerator was stamped on by a charging driver.

Jabouille left Renault at the end of 1980 for the Ligier team and was replaced by one Alain Prost who had driven for McLaren the year before, often eclipsing his team leader John Watson's performances there. Renault were on pole at Dijon, Silverstone, Hockenheim, Osterreichring, Zandvoort and Monza but even with the talented Prost at the wheel, only took the chequered flag at the French, Dutch and Italian Grand Prix. So, whilst Renault were very quick all season, lack of reliability cost them more wins. And thus 1981 was the year when the normally-aspirated Ford Cosworth engined Williams FW07C in the hands of Alan Jones and Carlos Reutemann slugged it out with Nelson Piquet's Brabham BT49C. Piquet's 50 points won the World Championship by just one point over Carlos Reutemann whose steady drives of that season amassed 49 points.

△ 1980 World Champion Alan Jones coming into the pits during practice for the British Grand Prix at Silverstone, 1981

▷ Carlos Reutemann and Frank Williams

△ Eddie Cheever being waved out of the pit lane for a timed practice run in the Tyrrell

The season gave Nigel Mansell his first serious break into Formula One when he was signed up alongside Elio de Angelis with Team Lotus.

1981 also was notable in that a third turbo contender entered the field – a small but well-organised and well-funded Toleman team which had competed with such success in the 1979 Formula Two Championship.

Owing to its inexperience in Formula One, however, the Toleman team could not persuade a major engine or turbo manufacturer to supply vital hardware. Toleman financed a Formula Two engine workshop, Brian Hart Ltd, to develop the motive power for the foray into Formula One. The cars were

▷ The late Colin Chapman, head of Team
Lotus

basically Formula Two with modifications to accommodate the revised twin-turbo powerplant.

The Brabham Team evaluated its BMW turbo engine during track testing of both the BT49 and BT50 cars. Consequently, Brabham fielded two turbo-engined cars for opener to the 1982 season in South Africa but after problems abandoned turbocharging until an ultimatum from BMW Motorsport forced Brabham to re-install a turbo engine in Piquet's car at the Belgian Grand Prix at Zolder. It was not until the British Grand Prix in July that the second car of Riccardo Patrese was again so equipped. Patrese had, after Kyalami, reverted

◁ Nelson Piquet, the Brazilian World Champion, drove Brabhams for more than half of the turbo decade

▷ An informal Carlos Reutemann in the paddock

△ The eyes of Mario Andretti prior to a race

◁ Andretti awaits the start of a race in his Alfa Romeo V12 179C

to the 'old faithful' Ford Cosworth. He won at Monaco while poor Nelson Piquet continued with his string of misfortunes. Piquet's only consolation was that shattering of Jonathan Palmer's unofficial 1 min 9.7 sec, Silverstone record with the turbo BT50 when he scored a 1 min 8.8 sec lap in May of that year.

The start of the 1982 season at Kyalami in January was a superb showing by Renault with the lighter and more compact RE30B. Alain Prost comfortably led the field until lap 41 when a slowly deflating rear tyre forced him to limp into the pits. Although the pits crew changed all four tyres in record quick time, Prost stormed back into the race in eigth place a lap behind Rene Arnoux who had inherited the lead. Quite simply, Prost in the Renault RE30B, probably the fastest car on the circuit, then put in one of his most stunning driving performances to unlap himself, gain on the other seven drivers in front of him and win the race by about 15 seconds.

△ The talented Gilles Villeneuve drove for Ferrari in the early eighties

▷ Gilles Villeneuve in conversation with the Ferrari team manager just before the start of the 1981 British Grand Prix at Silverstone

△ John Watson in the McLaren MP4/1 takes the chequered flag to win the 1981 British Grand Prix

◁◁ Watson on the start line

◁ The modest Grand Prix winner preferred '7-up' to champagne

▷▷ Renault turbos on pole. Arnoux and Prost were 1st and 2nd respectively on the grid at Silverstone in 1981

Shell Super Oil
Shell Super Oil
catnic
An
A.J.Gooding
Group
Shell Super Oil
Steel Building
Components
MICHELIN
16
europcar
RENAULT elf

△ Rene Arnoux explains a handling problem to the Renault Sport team manager, Gerard Larousse

▷ Renault Turbos of Arnoux and Prost streak away at the start of the 1981 British Grand Prix

South Africa was also notorious for bad tempered and ruthless politicking between FISA and FOCA – FISA being the motor sport regulating body and FOCA the Formula One Constructors' Association. No sooner had Prost won than FISA announced that all drivers' licences were suspended indefinitely, and the headlines featured this so prominently that the brilliant Frenchman's achievement was very underplayed. Renault ended the season by matching McLaren's four wins, Prost at South Africa and Brazil – Arnoux at France and Italy.

Both Ferrari and Renault further improved the fuel injection systems on their cars. Ferrari used a form of water injection emulsification and Renault with

△ Gilles Villeneuve in the turbocharged
Ferrari 126C of 1981

◁ Didier Pironi, the French driver for the
Ferrari team, 1980

a revised and very sophisticated electro-mechanical system that commanded variable pitch turbine blades.

Toleman and Hart further improved the performance of their engines steadily and with tyre up-rates as well, Warwick and Teo Fabi were in a better position than the Cosworth brigade. Derek Warwick conspicuously rewarded the team's efforts with a 119.22 mph fastest lap at Zandvoort driving the TG181B 'Belgrano' and was actually running second at the British Grand Prix before retiring.

For Ferrari, 1982 must be considered one of their most tragic seasons. At Zolder, Villeneuve going all out to try and set fastest lap in practice, came upon the much slower March driven by Jochen Mass. Somehow, the Ferrari's front wheel climbed over the March and catapulted Villeneuve's car to disaster. Villeneuve died in hospital and the whole of the motor racing scene was stunned. A fitting tribute came from Niki Lauda who reckoned he was 'the best in the business'.

Then at Hockenheim, with Didier Pironi leading the Championship with 39 points, came the second major Ferrari crash of the season. Pironi survived, but while Enzo Ferrari always said a Ferrari would be waiting for him when fully recovered, he was never to race cars again. Ironically, it was much later that he was to crash fatally in a powerboat race. Ferrari won the Constructors' Championship, although it was the Williams FW08 which took

▽ Alan Jones is arrested by crude catch fencing in front of the Silverstone grandstand. Villeneuve's Ferrari was unfortunately caught by the spinning Williams

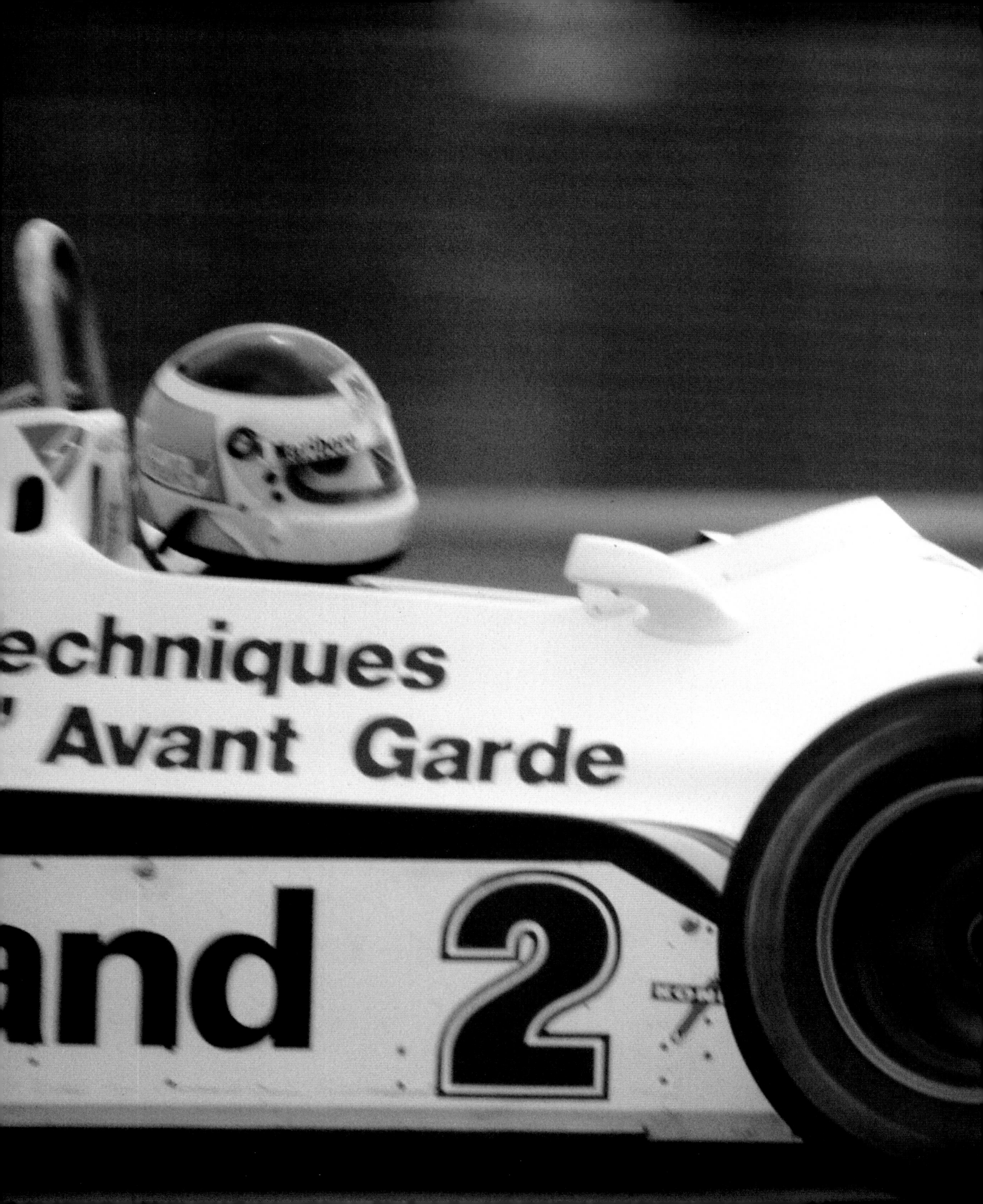
echniques
' Avant Garde
and
2

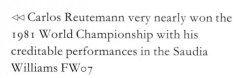
△ Slim Borgudd in the ATS D5 chasing
Eddie Cheever in the Tyrrell, 1981

◁◁ Carlos Reutemann very nearly won the
1981 World Championship with his
creditable performances in the Saudia
Williams FW07

Riccardo Patrese had to revert to a Cosworth
normally-aspirated engine until the BMW
turbocharged unit was made more reliable.
It was not until the 1982 British Grand Prix
that Patrese was re-installed in his Brabham
BT49 turbo seen here

△ Niki Lauda in the 1982 McLaren MP4/B

▷ Eddie Cheever driving Tyrrell No. 4 and Bruno Giacomelli in Alfa Romeo No. 23 storming through Paddock Bend at Brands Hatch, 1982

Keke Rosberg's to one win and many good 'places' and a well-deserved World Championship. In the author's opinion, Rosberg then and Nigel Mansell now, have much in common – style of driving, temperament and that tenacity to never give up.

Wings, and pit stops to refuel were all the rage in 1983 as they added to the drama and spectacle of the sport. The turbocharged cars were developing around 650 bhp and it was no longer competitive to run normally-aspirated cars. A turbo car, even allowing for the fact that it would consume more fuel, could run so much faster than a non-turbo that it could build up a substantial lead and actually make a quick pit stop to refuel and change its tyres, which was a

▷ Renault turbo RE30 with Alain Prost at wheel in 1982

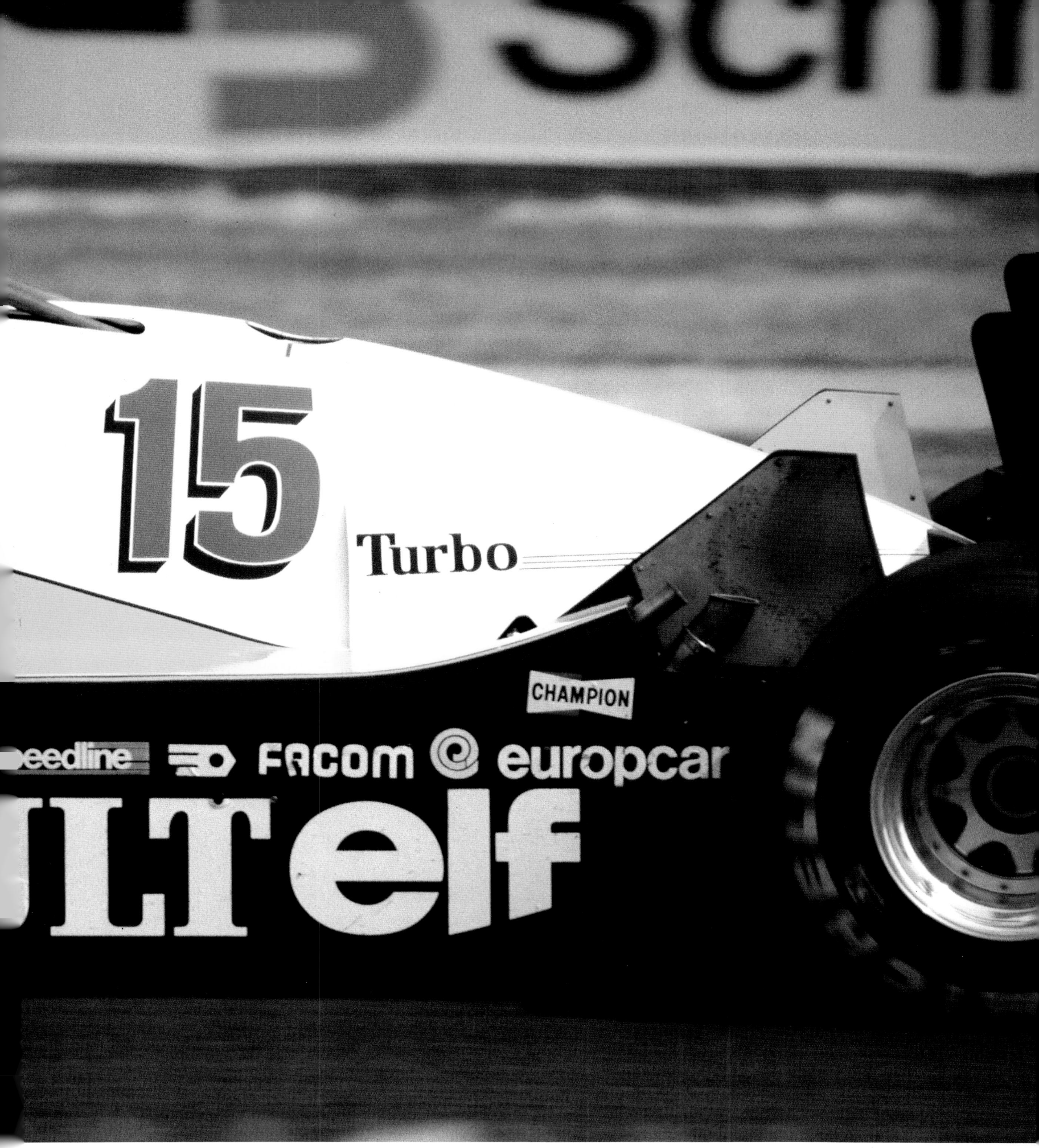
15
Turbo
CHAMPION
FACOM
europcar
elf

tremendous advantage on fast circuits. It was only on some of the slower circuits where the odds were more evenly matched. These pit stops proved very popular with both the spectator public and the teams although there were some misgivings about the aspect of safety and fire hazard during the refuelling operation. With the luxury of hindsight, these fears were not justified.

Another sensible improvement to stop cars attaining higher and higher speeds was the new FISA regulation that no full ground effects devices were to be allowed in 1983 and all cars had to have flat bottoms without any under-body aerodynamic tricks. Consequently, large wings and fins sprouted on the cars to compensate for the lack of the ground effect downforce.

Lotus, having survived the tragedy of the death of its founder, Colin Chapman in December 1982, developed its new 93T chassis and had installed in Elio de Angelis' car the powerful Renault V6 turbo engine. Newly appointed race director Peter Warr then announced that Nigel Mansell was to start the season with a Cosworth engine but he would be driving a Renault turbo later. Renault had a change in drivers – Arnoux split with Prost and went to Ferrari to partner Patrick Tambay. Eddie Cheever, the American driver, joined Prost as number two.

◁ Nigel Mansell's Lotus 94T was fitted with the Renault turbocharged engine late in 1983

▽◁ A mechanic carries out adjustments to the brake calipers on the 1983 JPS Lotus 94T

▽ Renault turbo engine of the Lotus 93T

◁ Patrick Tambay, the French Ferrari driver in 1983

▷ Rene Arnoux partnered Patrick Tambay at Ferrari in 1983

▽ Arnoux in the Ferrari at Druids Corner in the 1983 European Grand Prix at Brands Hatch

While the Ferrari of 1983 was much improved with water injection and a composite chassis, it had unproven drivers. Even so, the team won at San Marino, Montreal, Hockenheim and Zandvoort, which was enough to retain the Constructors' Championship.

This year the combination of Piquet with the very fast and sleek Brabham BT52 was the one to beat. In its latest form the engine was showing almost 750 bhp on the dynamometer. Designed by Gordon Murray it was built as a carbon fibre composite monocoque. Brabham also changed over from Goodyear crossply to Michelin radial tyres because it was believed that the newer car would handle better on radials. The weak point remained the unreliability of the BMW turbo engine. It was especially prone to failure in conditions where there was a rapid and then sustained rise in temperature.

Prost with the latest lighter and more efficient RE40 looked as though he was going to walk away with the Championship during the early races but the Brabham with Piquet driving very aggressively came from behind to take the lead and win his second World Championship title.

The normally-aspirated cars were totally outclassed and 1983 was the season when the non-turbo runners had to be really heroic to achieve any points. Keke Rosberg won brilliantly at Monaco even though all the odds were against

▷ Gordon Murray, designer of the Brabham BT52, talks to Nelson Piquet who has just come in after doing a fast lap in practice. Note the colourful Union Jack-like pattern on the ground beneath the car's nose

△ The extremely potent yet very unreliable BMW M-Power turbo engine which frustrated Piquet and Patrese

▽ The BMW turbo engine was also supplied to the 1983 ATS team. Here it is shown fitted to the ATS BMW D6

▷ ATS team mechanics pour fuel into a safety fuel can before the car can be refuelled

◁ A Renault crew member checks the tyre temperature on Eddie Cheever's turbocharged RE40 of 1983

△ Alain Prost, 1983

him. Daringly driving on slicks even though the surface was still damp but drying out, it was spectacular to see him race away from the rest of the field amidst clouds of spray.

When the Formula One circus was on the other side of the Atlantic John Watson, the veteran Ulsterman, 'out-Lauda'd' Lauda to drive from 22nd place on the grid to score a 1–2 win for McLaren at Long Beach, USA. With about 150 Grands Prix drives under his belt at the time he was the most experienced driver. Watson was quietly fast and understated but he ran in the shadow of Niki Lauda at McLaren. It was a tremendous pity that contractual problems deprived him of

◁ Aerodynamicist Frank Dernie taking note
of Rosberg's comments following a practice
lap. Brands Hatch, 1983

△ An active Frank Williams helping out with
a tyre change in the pits

◁ Keke Rosberg demonstrates a manoeuvre
to Frank Williams

◁ Keke Rosberg won his World Championship behind the wheel of a normally-aspirated predecessor of this Williams FW08C, but the handling of the raw turbocar prevented him from winning another Championship

△ Keke Rosberg and Patrick Head, 1983

▽ The cockpit of Keke Rosberg's Williams FW08C, 1983

◁ A Williams mechanic overhauls the
FW08C gearbox during a lunch break

△ 1983 Williams FW08C showing Cosworth
engine and disc brake set-up

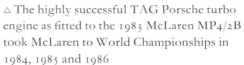

◁ The engine of Prost's McLaren is visible in the foreground while Lauda sits in car No. 8 beyond. Ron Dennis, the team head, can be seen in the background

△ The highly successful TAG Porsche turbo engine as fitted to the 1983 McLaren MP4/2B took McLaren to World Championships in 1984, 1985 and 1986

△ A Marlboro McLaren mechanic working on the disc brake unit of the MP4/1E

◁ John Watson (in the car) has a word for Ron Dennis

Player Grand F

△ Riccardo Patrese partnered Piquet at Brabham in the early days of the BMW turbo engine

◁ Winners rostrum, European Grand Prix, 1983. Piquet/Brabham won, followed by Prost/Renault and Mansell/Lotus

▷ The 1983 Tyrrells were decked-out in Benetton livery and car No. 3 was driven by Michele Alboreto. A team engineer takes notes while 'Uncle Ken' listens attentively to the driver's comments

Derek Warwick, in the Toleman TG183B
powered by a Hart turbo engine, had his fire
extinguisher go off accidentally during the
1983 European Grand Prix and had to retire
with frozen legs

△ Jean Pierre Jarier in the Ligier Gitanes during pit work at Silverstone practice, 1983

△◁ Candy Toleman bodyshells awaiting the 1983 TG183B chassis'

◁ The Arrows A6 of 1983 was driven by a relatively unknown Belgian, Thierry Boutsen

▷▷ The 1983 Spirit Honda 101 being refuelled

a drive in 1984, just when the TAG/Porsche turbo engine, having been introduced at Zandvoort in 1983, was giving the latest John Barnard designed McLaren MP-4 the urge to match its handling.

The other turbo runners for 1983 were Toleman with the newly re-designed TG183 shod with Pirelli tyres. Hart, who would have liked to have used the KKK turbo unit as used by the bigger teams, had been obliged to adopt an Anglo-American Garrett turbocharger for the practical reasons that the German KKK turbo manufacturers were not interested in supplying a small independent team. For the last few races of the season Hart located and used an Austrian Holset assembly which transformed the cars' reliability and it is questionable how Warwick and Fabi might have fared had these better turbochargers been available to the team from the beginning of the year.

Alfa Romeo with Andrea de Cesaris and Mauro Baldi ran two Alfa 183Ts with the engine producing enough power to keep up with the competition. However, it was so thirsty that the 200-litre fuel limit that was coming in 1984 was going to be a severe handicap to its chances of finishing races.

Finally for 1983, Honda, as a prelude to its later successful partnership with Williams, entered a car called the Spirit powered by a Honda V6 and driven by Stefan Johansson, the popular and amiable Swede. The Spirit made its maiden run at the British Grand Prix looking well-prepared and with aerodynamics rather like the Toleman. But it was plagued with turbocooler problems.

The Turbo comes of Age

Having had a year when the turbo-engined cars so totally dominated the racing scene, it is instructive to compare the situation in 1984 with the late 1950s and early 1960s when light but ingeniously designed cars by Colin Chapman and John Cooper, with inferior-powered Coventry Climax engines, driven by Stirling Moss, Jack Brabham and later Jim Clark, ran rings around the more potently equipped Ferraris, Maseratis and BRMs. The critical difference was the higher degree of engine/chassis integraton achieved by Chapman and Cooper. Similarly, although the turbos developed far more power it was not necessarily all transmitted to the driving wheels. In 1984 the Alfa Romeo V8, the BMW 4-cyl, the Ferrari V6, the Hart 4-cyl, the Honda V6, the Renault V6 and the Porsche V6 had the benefits of turbocharging. Cosworth DFV normally aspirated engines were still used only by Tyrrell and Arrows (while awaiting their BMW turbos), and were giving the turbocharged machinery a final race for its money.

Entering the new era of fuel efficiency, the turbos with their maximum 220-litre fuel limit, had to balance power output against economy using the turbo boost judiciously in order to last the full race distance. Motor sport enthusiasts became familiar with scenes of drivers often running out of fuel on final laps and cars being driven zig-zag to slosh the petrol about and to suck up the last drop from the tanks.

The top teams had very strong driver combinations. McLaren had Niki Lauda and Alain Prost. Williams paired Rosberg and Jacques Laffite and Brabham boasted Piquet and Teo Fabi. Renault, now with the new RE50 had fresh talent in Derek Warwick and Patrick Tambay, both consistently good, fast drivers, but Renault failed to win a single Grand Prix in 1984.

◁ The bodyshell comes off Nelson Piquet's 1985 Brabham BMW BT54 to expose the engine and chassis

▷▷ Piquet in the Brabham BMW BT54 desperately tries to beat a pole time set by Ayrton Senna in the Lotus Renault 97T

△ The very powerful Honda V6 turbo engine which powered the Williams cars of 1985 and 1986

◁ Keke Rosberg prepares himself before geting into the Williams Honda cockpit

It should not be forgotten that while 1984 was the year of the turbos, it was Williams' first year with the Honda V6 and Arrows had to wait for their BMW engine until mid-way through the season. A lot of lessons had to be learnt. It was easy enough to drop in a Honda turbo engine into a chassis designed for 200 bhp less but the resulting brute that emerged had monstrous handling. The Williams, for example, was wild to drive and only Keke Rosberg's abilty to control the FW09B gave him possibly the best victory of the season on a crumbling track in the blistering Dallas heat.

The other memorable race in 1984 for many race spectators was the rain-soaked Monaco Grand Prix. Alain Prost was leading in the McLaren but despite clouds of spray, Ayrton Senna, driving a fantastic race in the Toleman TG184 was catching him fast and was only three tenths of a second behind. The rain was

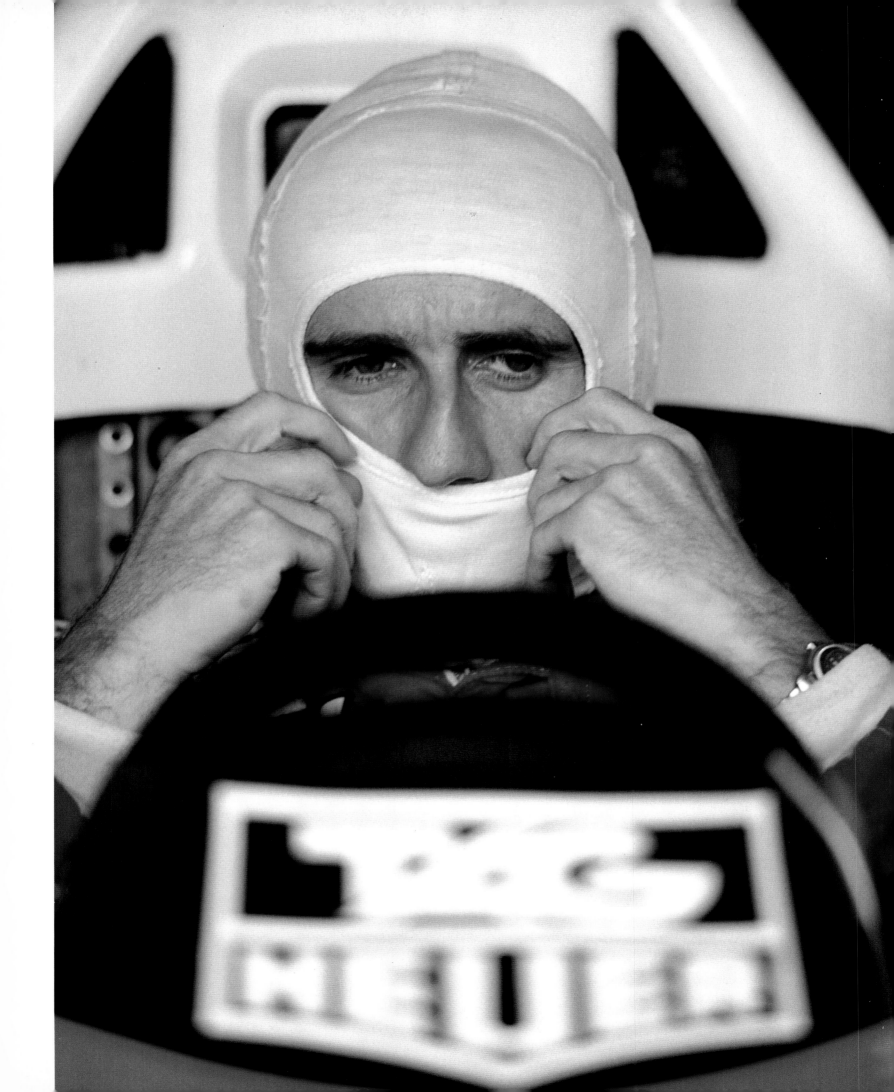

so heavy at that critical moment that Jacky Ickx, former World Champion and the Clerk of the Meeting at Monaco, took a wise and dispassionate decision to stop the race before full distance. The final positions were deemed to be the same as the race order at the time of the stoppage. Alain Prost won with only 4.5 points as the race was run for 31 laps only (less than half the total of 77 laps) and thus half the normal number of points were awarded to the first six runners. There was a very strong protest by the pro-Senna faction against the stoppage as it was felt that the race was conveniently stopped to save Prost being overtaken by Senna. On the contrary, if the race had not been abandoned and a serious incident resulted, Ickx would have been criticised for not using his powers to stop the race. Whichever way it is considered, there was no clear cut position, only better or worse solutions. In the author's opinion, Ickx acted prudently and quite properly even though he felt deprived at not being able to see the Prost versus Senna duel in the wet develop to a full crescendo.

Recent newcomers to Grand Prix racing could be forgiven if they believed that 1988 was the year of the first McLaren walkover, for this was the year when the red and white cars smashed all oppostion and won 15 out of 16 races with only Berger winning for Ferrari at Monza. It was in 1984 that McLaren originally dominated – Prost won seven Grand Prix and Lauda five, making a total of twelve wins out of sixteen. Yet with Prost's seven wins to Lauda's five, Niki Lauda scored half a point more and won the World Championship. There was tremendous sympathy for Prost but even though Prost was the consistently faster driver, whenever something went wrong he had either to retire or expire on the track, whereas Lauda managed to score points by driving carefully and tactically even in races where he was not victorious.

The off-circuit highlight of 1984 was the total ban on Ken Tyrrell's team by FISA after the German Grand Prix. Mystery still shrouds some aspects of the story but what is publicly known is that in order to extract every erg of power from the team's non-turbo Cosworth DFV engines Tyrrell adopted, at the Detroit Grand Prix earlier in the year, a form of water injection and undoubtedly had lead ballast in the water reservoir. Analysis revealed the water going into the injectors contained infinitesimal amounts of hydrocarbon deposits and this was shown to be clearly against the spirit of the regulations. Tyrrell protested and said that he was innocent, that the hydrocarbon could have been in the containers which were previously used for fuel and not properly cleaned out or that the Detroit tap water contained hydrocarbon deposits. The Tyrrell team appealed and obtained an injunction to let the cars take part as 'provisional' competitors in the forthcoming Grand Prix. However, the court of appeal later upheld the original ban and no Tyrrells ran in the last four Grand Prix. This was a terrible blow to a small team run on a shoestring. A lot of bad feeling prevailed with people taking sides and suspecting Tyrrell's motives for using the lead

◁◁ A thoughtful Ayrton Senna in 1985

◁◁ Alain Prost putting on his flame-proof balaclava, 1986

▷ Niki Lauda, nicknamed 'King Rat', was three times World Champion before he finally retired from Grand Prix racing in 1985

ballast were to bring up the cars' weight to the minimum 540 kg at the end of the race, which was absurd because the regulations permitted 'non-functional' weight to be carried. All that mattered was that the cars ended the meeting on or above the mark without anything being added after the chequered flag.

From the outset of the 1985 racing season, it looked as if the winning form of John Barnard's McLaren MP4/2 with the reliable and fuel-efficient TAG/Porsche engine would be the one for other teams to follow. The car had undergone minor refinements to improve an already successful and tested vehicle. Closed-season work eliminated any weak points that might have let the team down when stressed. Niki Lauda, now thrice World Champion, and Alain Prost were a formidable combination but Prost was now greatly more motivated to become the first French World Champion. The same could not be said for Lauda however, and less charitable observers remarked that his record-high 1985 driver's retainer was to be the down payment on another jetliner for Lauda Air. Whatever the validity of these claims Lauda provided some substance for them by driving in a manner less than befitting a World Champion in some of the races – he only finished in three that season. Lauda totally acquitted himself of these accusations by driving superbly at the Dutch Grand Prix, racing against

◁ A pit member about to jack-up Prost's McLaren in the pit lane during the 1985 season

▽ The McLaren MP4/2B brake disc and caliper layout of 1985

team-mate Prost in a lean and hungry display, ruthless in the way in which he kept Alain Prost at bay in the closing stages, taking the chequered flag to win his 25th and last Grand Prix victory. He announced his second retirement at the end of the year, as Prost won five races and went on to win his well-deserved Championship with 73 points totalled from his eleven best scores.

FISA regulations further reduced fuel capacity from 220 litres to 195 litres. Overnight the engine management specialists were confronted with an even tougher challenge in the quest for fuel efficiency. As expected, the teams which stayed on top of these new regulations were significantly the same which mastered the demands of the earlier limit.

◁ Alain Prost clinched his 1985 World Championship title to become the first French World Champion after almost thirty years

▽ Prost showers the crowd with champagne, as is the done thing

▷▷ Mansell's Williams FW10/10B bottoms before Hailwood Hill showering sparks from the titanium undershield

Williams, with the FW10 which had matured from the ill-handling car of the previous year, was one of the front-runners in 1985. The Honda V6 still provided urge in a sudden burst of torque at high rpm. Smoothness in power delivery was not achieved until mid-season when Honda modified the stroke of the engine and this made the cars extremely competitive in terms of power, controllability and fuel efficiency. It was sheer pleasure to see the extrovert Rosberg in full flight during qualifying at the British Grand Prix at Silverstone when he recorded the fastest ever lap at a speed of 160.938 mph. Williams won four Grand Prix with Rosberg's splendid win at Detroit and also in Australia – Mansell scored his first Formula One victory at the Grand Prix d'Europe at Brands Hatch and then underlined it by winning at Kyalami in South Africa.

It was a dismal year for Alfa Romeo and, to a lesser extent, Ferrari. Alfa abandoned its new 185T in favour of an improved version of the 184T with slight modifications, which was to be dubbed the 184TB. Its handling was acceptable although power output was not exactly scintillating. It could have been competitive but for the number of turbo failures suffered all season and it was no surprise that Alfa Romeo withdrew from racing for 1986. Ferrari started with quite a well-handling, Harvey Postlethwaite designed 156/85. It was driven by Michele Alboreto and Rene Arnoux, and for the latter part of the season, Stefan Johannson. Although Alboreto drove consistently throughout, winning at Montreal and Nurburgring, the Ferrari's performance was gradually being outclassed by the other frontline teams, especially McLaren and Williams. Even so, Ferrari ended up scoring 82 points to McLaren's 90 to win second place in the Constructors' Championship.

Renault, the turbo pioneers, had a new chassis in the RE60. Both Tambay and Warwick found it to be slower than the older RE50. Management changes at Renault Sport resulted in muddled decisions that confronted the team's engineers and designers with conflicting priorities. The departure of Gerard Larousse to Ligier, lack of morale, and the disappointing performance of the Renault cars led the company to announce the departure of Renault Sport from the scene at the end of the season. Renault Sport, however, guaranteed a supply of their engines to Lotus and other teams who had contracts with them.

Team Lotus, which had earlier recruited Gerard Ducarouge, the talented ex-Alfa Romeo chief engineer, produced the highly competitive 97T. Handling

▷ Nigel Mansell drives a dominating race to win the 1985 European Grand Prix in his Williams FW10/10B. This was his first-ever Grand Prix win

▷▷ Mansell/Williams at the top of Hailwood Hill in the 1985 European Grand Prix at Brands Hatch

△ Michele Alboreto put in consistent
performances for Ferrari in 1985

▷ A frantic pit stop and tyre change for
Johannson's Ferrari

▷▷ Michele Alboreto's turbocharger fails
spectacularly during timed practice before
the 1985 European Grand Prix

△ Nelson Piquet in the Brabham BT54 about   ▷ Stefan Johannson in the Ferrari 156/85
to overtake Philippe Alliot in the Skoal
Bandit March RAM03 Hart, 1985

was amongst the best of the 1985 cars and Ayrton Senna, now driving for Lotus after his acrimonious and much publicised departure from Toleman, was driving brilliantly, winning the very wet Portuguese Grand Prix and the Belgian Grand Prix at Spa. But it was still the unreliability, lack of ultimate power and unpredictable fuel consumption that prevented this partnership from winning more races.

The 1986 season saw more driver changes. Piquet, after winning only at Paul Ricard in 1985 and probably fed up with the politics of the tyre companies coupled to machine unreliablity that could not let him win more than once even with 1200 bhp at his disposal, signed for Frank Williams. Bernie Ecclestone had tried to haggle with Piquet over his 1986 retainer and although he had won two World Championships with Brabham he felt this was personally just unbearable. Rosberg had slotted into Niki Lauda's seat at McLaren alongside the new World Champion Alain Prost. On paper the combination of Rosberg and McLaren appeared unbeatable. But inexplicably the magic of Rosberg/Williams was never repeated despite solid results. McLaren car and team were efficient machines that were not designed to be driven with bravura as was Rosberg's temperament.

▽ Derek Warwick also drove for Renault in 1985, but the Renaults were uncompetitive and the French team left the Formula 1 scene at season's end

▷ Patrick Tambay also had a frustrating season in 1985, driving the Renault RE60

◁ The bodyshell of Senna's Lotus 97T being lowered onto the chassis prior to the start of the European Grand Prix, 1985

△ Ayrton Senna in the 1985 Lotus Renault 97T which he drove inspiringly when the engine ran well

◁ JPS Team Lotus mechanics await Ayrton
Senna's Lotus 97T in the pits

▷▷ Jonathan Palmer's Zakspeed belching-out
turbo flames from the exhaust

△ A Williams Honda being examined by the scrutineers at the end of a timed practice lap

If 1984 and 1985 were vintage McLaren, 1986 was very definitely a Williams/Honda benefit. The team started the year on a very low note with Frank Williams sustaining injuries in a road accident in France that left him partially paralysed and hospitalised. However the team, under the capable direction of Patrick Head capitalised on all its experience of the previous season and in the FW11 had an extremely potent challenger. There was no other engine as powerful as the Honda and none was more able to transfer this power to the track than the Williams. Between Piquet and Mansell the cars clocked up nine wins, and everyone thought one of the Williams drivers was headed for the Championship. Yet, with Mansell's five wins and Piquet's four, it was Prost who

△ Nigel Mansell in unfamiliar clothes

▷ Mansell and Frank Dernie of Williams
discuss race tactics

won the Championship for the second time running by his four wins and consistency in finishing and scoring vital Championship points. It was a very closely run Championship – Prost with 72, Mansell 70 and Piquet with 69 points. The moral victor of the year was Mansell, having driven superbly all season with verve and maturity only to have it all blown away with a spectacular burst tyre at Adelaide amidst the groans of millions of ardent TV viewers. Of course Williams won the Constructors' Championship with a massive lead but that was small consolation to Mansell in his disappointment.

In terms of personal relationships between the drivers, it was interesting to see how Mansell relaxed by playing golf with his arch rival Prost, whereas there was an atmosphere of tenseness and mistrust between him and his own team-mate Piquet.

The only other team in contention in 1986 was Lotus, using a more powerful Renault engine. Ayrton Senna's prodigious talent took them to eight pole positions and victories in Jerez and Detroit despite nagging unreliability.

Gerhard Berger, the young Austrian driver, fearless and charging almost in the same mould of Niki Lauda in his early days at Ferrari, took the Rory Byrne designed Benetton BMW Turbo to a well-earned win at Mexico. Teo Fabi in a similar car was on pole in Austria where he also set the fastest lap during the race. Ferrari rushed the new 850 bhp F186 onto the starting grids but although testing showed it to be fast it did not figure higher than a second place for Alboreto in the Austrian Grand Prix at Oesterreichring and several third places for Stefan Johannson.

Sadly for Brabham, the Formula One fraternity lost one of its most gifted drivers when Elio de Angelis was fatally injured in a crash during testing at the Paul Ricard circuit in the South of France near Le Castellet. Brabham's low-drag BT55 fitted with a slimline BMW M12/13 engine and Pirelli tyres looked exciting and promised to deliver. Overheating, and gearbox failures on the Pete Weissman designed 7-speed box meant that the highest places achieved this season by Riccardo Patrese were sixth at San Marino and Detroit.

Ford unveiled its long-awaited new turbocharged V6 Grand Prix engine that it had developed in association with Cosworth Engineering. Of very compact dimensions it was installed in the all-new Team Haas Lola sponsored by Beatrice Foods. This new team, with Ford's backing, was instrumental in seducing Alan Jones back onto the Formula One grid from retirement. The

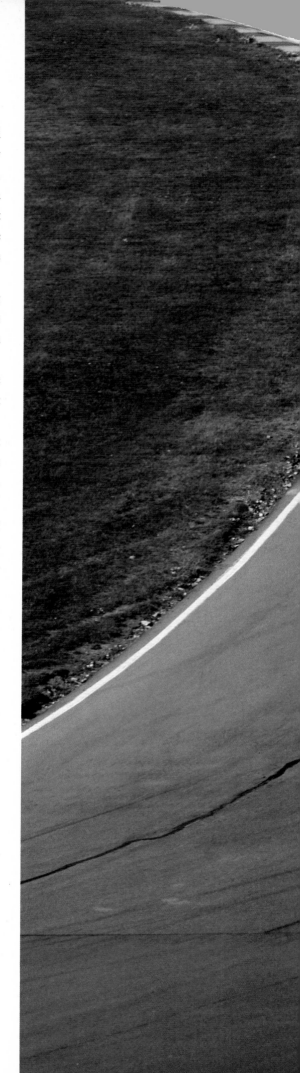

▷ Alboreto in the Ferrari 156/85 chases one of the Tyrrells

◁ The very talented Elio de Angelis, who died tragically in 1986

Prost and Rosberg, when they were team-mates at McLaren

◁ Refuelling operation on Senna's JPS Lotus
98T of 1986

▷ The Ayrton Senna/Lotus partnership came
to an end in 1987 when Senna was invited to
join McLaren

▽ The Renault turbo engine, as installed in
the 1986 Lotus 98T, gave good power but
was rather unreliable

second driver for this immaculately organised team was Patrick Tambay, who had been left without a drive after two pretty frustrating years with Renault Sport when they withdrew from Formula One as a team.

On the engine front, Renault apparently breached its exclusive two year contract with Team Lotus by supplying engines to the Tyrrell team. Lotus was waiting for a chance to opt for the Honda V6 which was available to them in 1987 on the *proviso* that the team took on as one of its drivers the Japanese Satoru Nakajima. Lotus agreed to this and ended its relationship with Renault, who in turn found themselves only servicing Tyrrell, a second division team without top grade drivers. Thus, the pioneers of the turbo era took the sad decision to end their Formula One turbo engine programme.

◁ Beatrice-sponsored Lola Ford with Alan Jones at the wheel

▽ Alan Jones, World Champion in 1981, was lured back from retirement to drive the new Beatrice-sponsored Lola Ford in 1986

△ Honda technician preparing a substitute
V6 turbo engine for the Williams FW11

▷ Nigel Mansell and Patrick Head check
practice times on the TV monitor whilst
mechanics carry out adjustments to the car

◁◁ The line-up at the start of the 1986 British Grand Prix. This was the second start following a pile-up which stopped the race in its first lap

△ Stefan Johannson was recruited by Ferrari in 1986

▷ Johannson's Ferrari being pushed back into the pits from the starting grid after failing to start at the British Grand Prix, 1986

▷▷ At the morning's untimed warm-up, Michele Alboreto comes in for de-briefing and reports on the car's performance

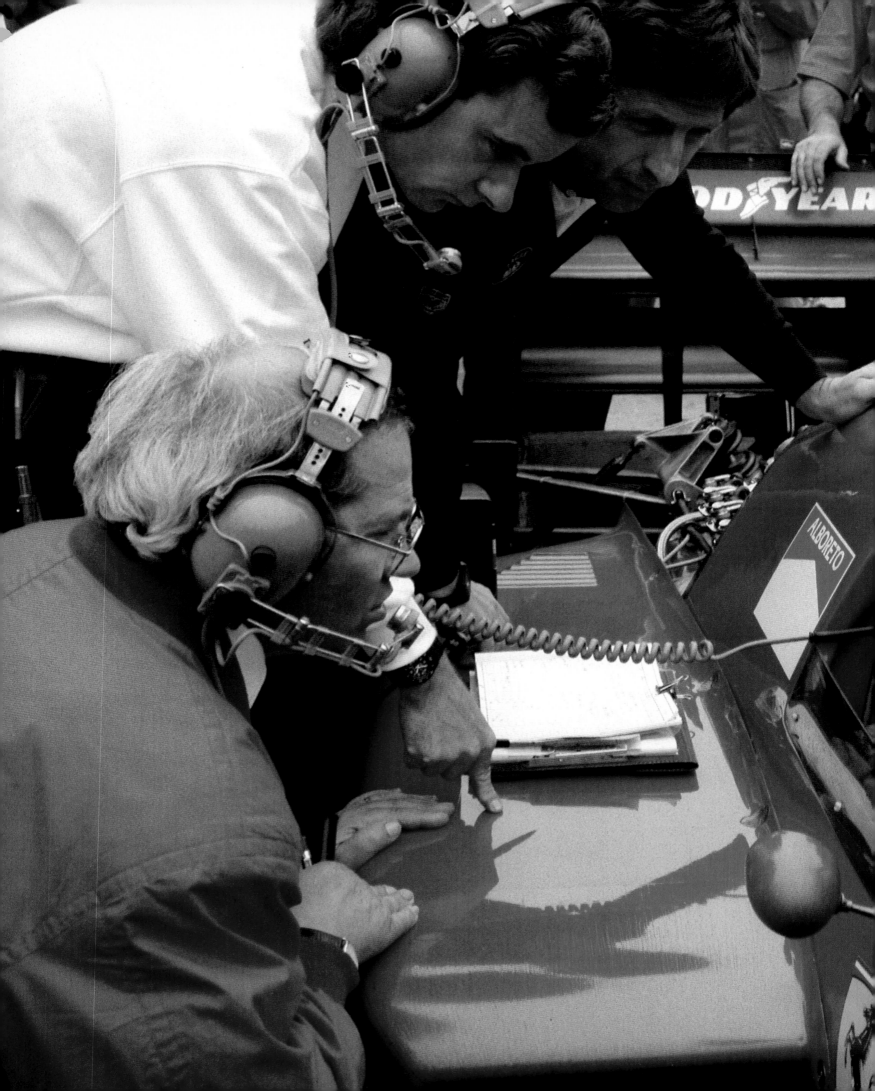

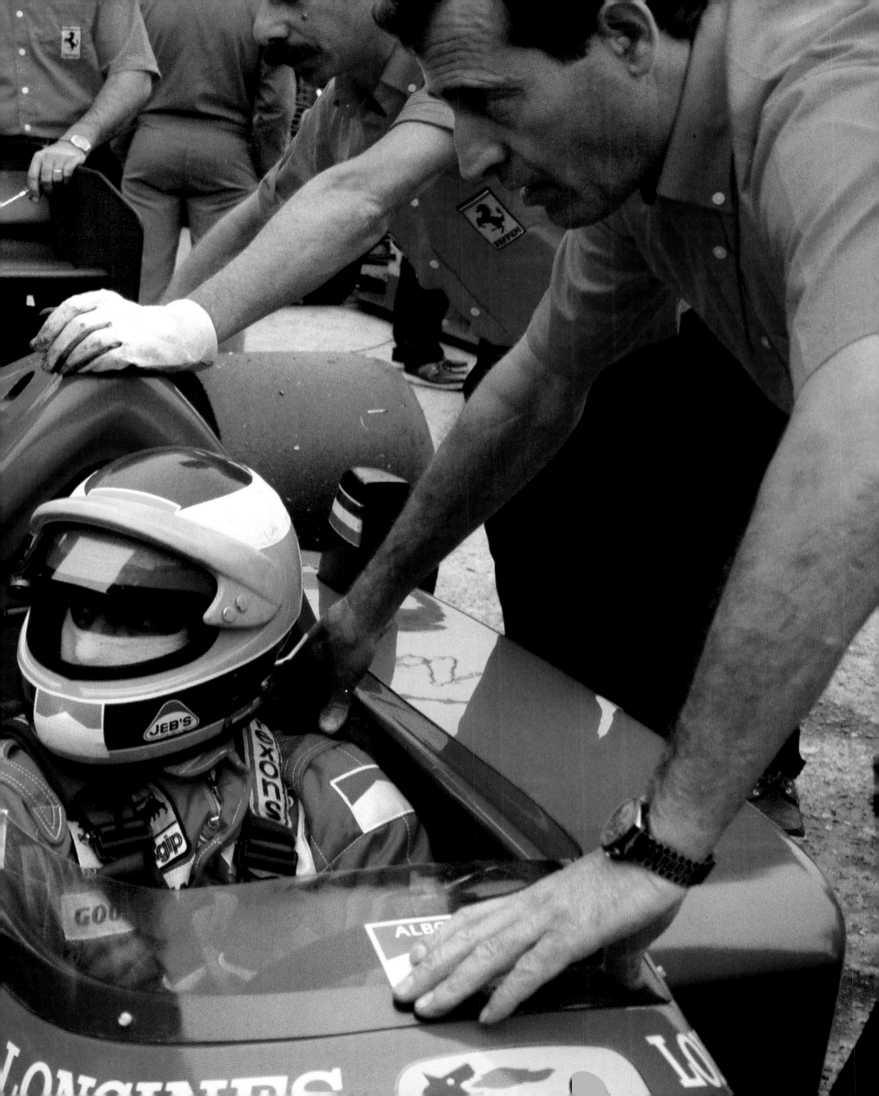

⊲ Gerhard Berger, the Austrian driver, was in the Benetton seat in 1986

▷ Berger, with injured right hand, points out a defective seat belt mounting to a Benetton engineer

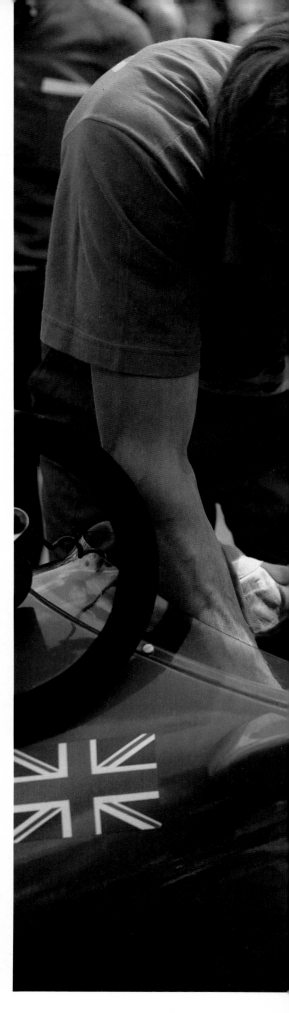

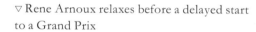

▽ Rene Arnoux relaxes before a delayed start to a Grand Prix

△ Cockpit of the McLaren MP4/2C TAG turbo of 1986

◁ Keke Rosberg switched to McLaren in 1986

◁◁ The smooth and fluent style of World Champion Alain Prost shows as he goes around a tight bend in McLaren No. 1

▷ The TAG Porsche turbo engine of 1986, as fitted to the McLaren MP4/2C, was overshadowed by the power of the Honda V6 turbo. But, thanks to Prost's consistent driving and Mansell's bad luck in Adelaide, the engine secured McLaren and Prost the 1986 World Championship

◁◁ Cheering crowds spur Mansell on to victory in the closing laps of the 1986 British Grand Prix. Piquet started from pole in his Williams Honda FW11 and led the race up to lap 23 before Mansell overtook him and led to the finish

▷ Nigel Mansell's face tells the whole story of his British Grand Prix victory in 1986

◁▽ Nigel Mansell and his wife, Rosanne

△ John Barnard and Alain Prost during
practice. The two drivers struck a
partnership that paid-off in Championship
wins

▷ The McLaren MP4/2C driven by Alain
Prost won the Frenchman his second
consecutive World Championship in 1986

Turbo Swansong

To limit power and speed, FISA introduced a new regulation in 1987 that made it mandatory to fit boost control valves or 'pop off' valves as they were referred to popularly.

Williams started the 1987 season where the previous year left off with the FW11B, a revised version of the extremely successful 1986 car. Patrick Head's active-ride Williams gave Piquet an excellent win at Monza but when Mansell, using the passive-ride FW11B beat it convincingly at Jerez during the Spanish Grand Prix, Williams made the decision to continue with the tried and tested FW11B for the last few races of the year. The Championship tussle for the 1987 season was in many ways similar to 1984. Remember, Alain Prost had his seven brilliant wins, yet Niki Lauda still walked away with the title. Well, it was Nigel Mansell this season running rings around the theoretical number one driver at Williams – Nelson Piquet. Yet Piquet, with his three wins to Mansell's six, took the title playing the Championship game in the same way as Niki Lauda used the system, and was also lucky enough to inherit a few victories, unlike the Austrian. Bad luck too played its part in Mansell not being on the Championship podium. Tangling with Senna at Spa and a wheelnut working loose at the Hungaroring lost him two possible wins. And to top it all, a spine injury caused by a pile-up at Suzuka in Japan prevented him from participating in the Australian Grand Prix. The Williams Honda was unbeatable and uncatchable and apart from a couple of silly breakdowns was extremely reliable. It was a great pity that the successful Honda/Williams partnership, owing to politics and Frank William's refusal to play the Honda tune, was not continued for 1988.

Prost, with the post-Barnard McLaren powered by the final version of the TAG/Porsche engine, kept up with the Williams Hondas and won three Grand Prix this year. Without doubt, Prost, now with 28 Grand Prix wins

◁ Nelson Piquet, driving the last turbocharged Williams Honda, won his third World Championship in 1987 with less wins than his team-mate Mansell but more consistent performances

behind him, was the most 'complete', all-rounder and if such a person exists, the best driver of the 1980s.

Things were different at McLaren, John Barnard had left to start Ferrari's UK-based GTO operation and Steve Nichols had taken over from him. Keke Rosberg had retired and Johannson was his replacement. Ron Dennis still controlled McLaren as a model of efficiency and the last word in preparation.

Senna's commitment at Lotus was exemplary, but the actively suspended car won only twice – at Monaco and Detroit. And only when Mansell, who was leading, retired.

The likeable Berger, at Ferrari now, had matured since his Benetton days and in the opinion of many observers was among the top echelon of the quickest drivers. He won twice – at Suzuka and at Adelaide. On both occasions he displayed superb flair. Given the improving competitiveness of the F187 he was certainly looking like a future Champion.

△ On a full fuel tank Alain Prost bottoms the titanium undershield of the 1987 McLaren creating a spectacular fireworks display

▷ The 'Professor', Alain Prost. Probably the most refined and complete all-round driver of the eighties, now three times World Champion and an all-time record holder with over forty Grand Prix wins

▷▷ Ayrton Senna sits patiently in the Lotus Honda of 1987 in its brilliant yellow Camel colours

Benetton switched to the recently introduced Ford engine that made its debut in 1986. The Benetton Ford B187 was a very neat, aerodynamic machine, benefiting from the small dimensions of the Ford Cosworth engine. After a hesitant start with the inexperienced Lola Haas team in 1986 the Ford Cosworth Turbo engine was becoming a force to be reckoned with. Under the maximum 4.0 bar boost limit of 1987 it was developing almost 1000 bhp at the end of the season and turbo lag had almost been eradicated. Both Teo Fabi and Thierry Boutsen were impressive in their first tests with the new car – Fabi was fastest of all in the Rio tests – an extremely competitive car/driver package which looked set to give Rory Byrne and his team good placings at least, if not outright wins, in 1987.

The Brabham team had had a couple of bad years and 1987 was no better. Without Piquet, and later Gordon Murray, Patrese worked hard with a moderately reliable car with a disappointing engine but still produced a few respectable finishes. The team was going downhill, however, and Patrese moved to Williams at the end of the year as Mansell's number two.

▷ Nelson Piquet was Nigel Mansell's team-mate in 1986 at Williams and won his third World Championship in 1987

▽ A pit crew member fastens Piquet's safety harness prior to a practice session

Arrows, also with BMW engines and a bit more funding, made a concerted effort this year to extract more performance from its cars. Derek Warwick and Eddie Cheever drove hard but the technical superiority and resources of the top-class turbo teams were such that they found it difficult to qualify anywhere near the front.

Finally, Tyrrell and March, ran with normally aspirated engines in anticipation of the new formula in 1989. Both teams used the trusty Cosworth DFZ prepared and serviced by Brian Hart Ltd, who were now part of the Cosworth Group. There was a dangerously wide power gap between the Cosworth producing around 575 bhp and the most powerful turbos producing twice that figure. The speed differential between these two classes of runners provided some hairy moments as the faster cars were baulked by the Cosworth-powered teams and other slower machines. Inevitably this gave rise to a debate as to whether the two formulae should be competing side by side.

Jonathan Palmer, in the Tyrrell, drove consistently and clinched the Jim Clark Championship for the normally aspirated class.

◁△ Nigel Mansell talks to friend Greg Norman, the golfing champion, before the start of the British Grand Prix at Silverstone in 1987

△ The carbon fibre disc brake arrangement on the 1987 Canon Williams Honda FW11B. Note the cooling ducts

▷ A sea of tyres being prepared for a race weekend by a specialist member of the Ligiers Gitanes crew

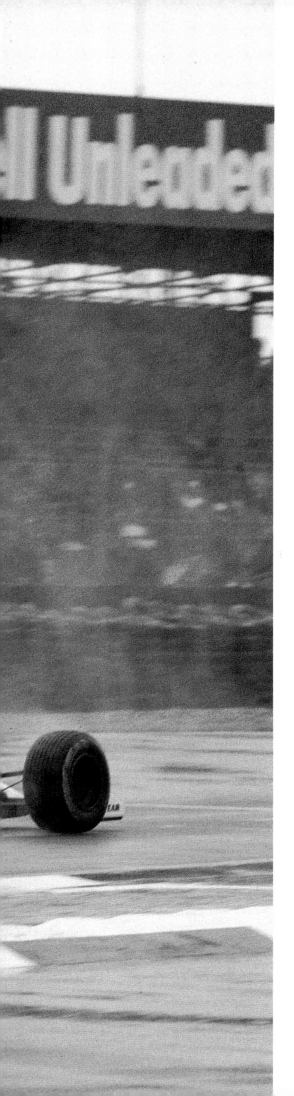

The Final Year, 1988

In the countdown to the new, normally aspirated 3.5-litre formula for 1989, the maximum permitted turbo boost was cut from 4.0 bar to a 2.5 maximum and the fuel limit was reduced by 45 litres to 150 litres. The non-turbos had no fuel limit and were allowed the advantage of being lighter at 500 kg as opposed to the turbo's minimum weight limit of 540 kg. To even out matters further, drivers of the turbo brigade complained of the way the pop off valves cut off the boost abruptly when nearing the 2.5 bar boost. So on paper it looked as if the domination of the turbo's reign would be curbed at last and that the majority of teams would now opt for the non-turbo route. The better, normally aspirated teams were expected to give the turbos a hard time. 1988 promised to be the most openly contested Grand Prix season in years.

Of the major turbo teams, McLaren's MP4/4s were now equipped with an advance-generation Honda V6, replacing the now venerable TAG/Porsche engine. Lotus' aerodynamic 100T had use of the same basic Honda V6. Ferrari's latest F187/V6 with redesigned cylinder heads was much improved through wind-tunnel testing during the latter part of the 1987 season and was showing much promise which paralleled their revived fortunes. Arrows were still with the Megatron developed BMW and West Zakspeed were the only Ford Cosworth turbo runners. Lastly, it is worth mentioning that Alfa Romeo's hopelessly outmoded V8 turbo was still being used by Osella.

And behind came the non-turbos. The Williams team used John Judd prepared Honda-based V8 engines that delivered adequate, smooth power in their latest Frank Dernie designed FW12 chassis with active-ride suspension. The March Racing team also used Judd engines in their sleek looking March 881 which was designed by Adrian Newey. Ligier, with the JS31, was the third team to use the Judd engine.

The conditions at the 1988 British Grand Prix at Silverstone were such that it took brave men like Berger, Mansell and Senna, seen here, to race through the blinding spray thrown up by the cars in front

Cosworth's slightly revised and marginally more powerful engine, designated DFR, was employed by Benetton in its B188, and by Tyrrell in the 017, besides other smaller teams such as the Larousse Calmels Lola, Minardi, AGS, Coloni, Rial, Euro Brun and Scuderia Italia.

As for the drivers, McLaren had the superlative duo of Alain Prost and Ayrton Senna. Williams had Nigel Mansell and Riccardo Patrese. Lotus looked to a good season with Nelson Piquet and Satoru Nakajima. Alessandro Nannini and Thierry Boutsen drove the Benettons. Alboreto and Berger continued with Ferrari. Mauricio Gugelmin and Ivan Capelli at March were intelligent and promising young drivers, both fast and smooth.

In the final year of the turbo era, it was the McLaren steamroller that won every race but one in the calendar. The season became a contest between the two McLarens. There were two races run within each race – one between the McLarens and one between all the other cars. As was to be expected Ayrton Senna, driving with aggression, determination and ruthlessness was a well-deserved Champion. Nobody in Formula One was hungrier for the Championship and no one it seemed, could have deprived him of it this year, with 13 pole positions and eight wins. Prost actually scored an amazing 105 points but as he could only count eleven best results, had to dop to 87. Senna, with 94 points had to drop only 4 and ended with 90. The McLaren team won the Constructors' Championship with an unprecedented record of 199 points. Another record was set by Prost as the total number of his Grand Prix victories rose to 35, raising the status of the thrice World Champion to that of an all-time great. This crushing demonstration of McLaren's superiority overshadowed everything. Ferrari's prestigious Italian Grand Prix victory with Berger winning and Alboreto coming second was perhaps some small compensation for the *Tifosi*, as the Italian fans are known, still grieving at the death of the *Commendatore*, the legendary Enzo Ferrari, just four weeks before.

Nigel Mansell in the Judd powered Williams had a very frustrating season with overheating and electronic bugbears. Even then, in the face of all odds he never gave up, always scored 105 per cent for effort, and put Senna under tremendous pressure in the wet at Silverstone, coming a splendidly deserved second and setting the fastest lap of the race during the chase.

Gerhard Berger's qualities as a racer had blossomed in 1987 and he was the only driver to have won a really well-deserved Grand Prix in 1988 apart from the McLaren twins. He showed true form at Monaco where he was second to Prost and in Mexico where he had to back off from attacking Senna to conserve fuel after being mislead by a faulty read-out from the fuel gauge in his Ferrari. He even snatched pole position from Senna at the very fast Silverstone circuit for the British Grand Prix and led in the streaming wet conditions for 14 laps before he had to concede to another nemesis – the appalling fuel consumption of the F187/88C.

△ Mansell shaved off his moustache in 1988 – possibly a reaction to his disappointment with the Judd V8 engine . . .

▷ A top view of the Williams FW12 showing the V8 Judd normally-aspirated engine that Williams used in 1988, the last year of the turbo era

◁ The ever-popular Nigel Mansell signs programmes for his fans

Nelson Piquet had a dreadful year with really trailing performances in the Lotus Honda, powered by an engine that was by rational standards of comparison, equal to those used by McLaren. There were suggestions in some quarters that Honda was supplying specially prepared engines to McLaren but when Honda heard these rumours they promptly offered Lotus their choice of engines from the whole production batch. A more likely answer to the team's uncompetitiveness was probably driver motivation and a lack of coordination made worse by the team's low morale. Piquet's frustration was made all the more galling by the 'hype' in the media that the Lotus that was to have been the salvation of his undisputed number one status. His uncharacteristic remarks about Nigel and Rosanne Mansell were most unworthy of a World Champion. Even the novice Nakajima gave Piquet a run for his money on occasion. All-in-all it was a wasted year for both Lotus and Piquet – best forgotten.

Thierry Boutsen and Alessandro Nannini were very strong runners at Benetton, the team being placed third in the Constructors' Championship.

▽ In the McLaren paddock area, tyres are kept at their most effective temperature by electrically-heated blankets powered by generators

▷ Ayrton Senna's McLaren MP4/4 and
Nelson Piquet's Lotus Honda 100T seen
from above during a practice session in 1988
at Silverstone

◁ Thierry Boutsen, the Belgian driver who partnered Alessandro Nannini during 1988, seen in the Benetton Ford B188

◁▽ Nigel Mansell in the Judd powered Williams FW12

▽ Michele Alboreto, a Ferrari driver in 1988

Boutsen's style was smooth, precise yet quick, but somehow lacked the aggression of a Senna or Berger. Nannini was a 'discovery' in that he was an extremely brisk driver when the mood took him as was seen in his performance at Monza before misfortune struck in the form of a throttle sensor failure.

Ivan Capelli and Mauricio Gugelmin were both good at putting their Marches in contention against much more potent machinery. It was enthralling to see Capelli actually squeezing past Prost and leading the Japanese Grand Prix, albeit momentarily.

Tyrrell had an awful year, the only highlight being Jonathan Palmer's fifth place at Monaco. Arrows had a slightly better year than 1987, Cheever scoring third place at Monza – its best-ever result.

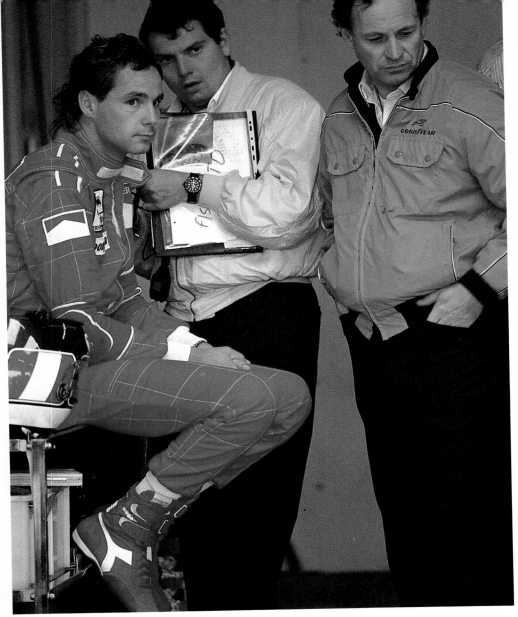

◁ Gerhard Berger (left) signed for Ferrari in 1988

▷ Practice session, Silverstone, 1988. The cars are seen joining from the pit lane at Copse Corner

▽ Gerhard Berger in the Ferrari 187/88C

Some commentators would say that McLarens were so much superior in everything this season. Others would equally argue that while McLaren got everything right first time the competition always managed to get something wrong somehow. Just as emphatically Prost and McLaren won the first Grand Prix of the season in Brazil, the same combination ended the turbo decade in the last Grand Prix of the year in Adelaide, with Prost first and Senna second, stamping their authority over their peers in a fitting flourish – the manner of which may never again be seen in the history of Formula One Grand Prix racing.

In summing up the period from 1979 to 1988, there are several factors to consider. Cost: Formula One Grand Prix motor racing has always been expensive in terms of machinery, technology and talent. As the sport became more and more sophisticated, the cost escalated in proportion. The introduction of the turbocharged engine into the Formula One scene increased enormously the costs of technical development needed to overcome the turbo's drawbacks: heat, thirst, weight and controllability.

As more and more power was extracted from the engines, the machinery was subjected to higher stresses and the reliability of transmissions, driveshafts, brakes and chassis' was bound to suffer. Consequently these problems also had to be resolved if a team wished to stay competitive. Honda reputedly spent about £20m on the development of their extremely successful V6 turbo engine that so dominated the final three years of the turbo decade, powering the Williams and McLaren cars and drivers to their respective World Championships.

Currently, the overall annual budget for a first rank Formula One team would be in excess of £7m. The teams in turn have to recoup the finance from major sponsors such as Shell, Marlboro, Elf, Benetton, Fosters, Canon, and others who naturally spend these vast amounts of money in return for the tremendous publicity afforded them by the television coverage of Grand Prix racing. The most prominent figure, who had the foresight to encourage sponsorships and make this possible, is Bernie Ecclestone. In creating FOCA, he managed to generate media deals of ·mind-boggling proportions and thus guaranteed the sponsors enormous publicity via worldwide broadcasting.

The increase in speed and power created a new breed of driver. Enthusiastic and carefree amateurism has been ruthlessly cast aside in favour of business-like professionalism. Unless prodigiously talented, a would-be driver in recent times must bring large amounts of sponsorship money to his chosen team in order to be considered for a drive.

▷ A wet start to a Grand Prix. Mauricio Gugelmin in the March Judd 881 pictured on the start line at the British Grand Prix of 1988

◁ Alain Prost, 1988

▷ Heated tyre blankets keep the temperature of Senna's McLaren tyres to the optimum level for maximum grip

▽ Ayrton Senna, 1988

The technology involved in the development of Grand Prix cars is ever improving and at any given moment is at the very zenith of 'state of the art' design and practice. With aerodynamicists employing wind tunnels and hi-tech engineers using space programme-type materials, the know-how emerging from Formula One research can only benefit the ordinary road car manufacturers and, in turn, we the road users.

◁ Nigel Mansell in the underpowered Williams Judd FW12 drove a superb race in the wet to challenge Senna for the lead but eventually had to settle for second place. Silverstone, 1988

△ Berger leading Senna in the early stages of the 1988 British Grand Prix at Silverstone

▽ Ayrton Senna drove impeccably in the atrocious conditions to win the 1988 British Grand Prix

▷▷ The art of spectating . . .